"My biggest goal for my books is that they spread the love of Jesus in a way that every child can connect to. My dream is for every kid to be introduced to the hope and love of Jesus. Therefore, a portion of the profits made from this book will go directly to spreading the light of Jesus, to children in need, all across the world."

Jess

My Brother the Angel

Written and Illustrated
By Jess Owen

Dedicated to all the angels

Mama has a surprise,
she says it's for me.

It lives in her tummy,
that I'll later see.

She says it's a boy,
and I'll be a sissy.

I'm full of joy,
so I give her a kissy!

I wonder how he'll look,
if he'll have a good heart.

I draw us together,
and hang up the art.

I ask when he'll come,
mama says soon.

He'll be out of her tum,
the very next June.

The day will be sweet,
like no other

When I finally meet,
my new little brother.

Then one day,
mama has cried.

And she tells me,
"Our lil boy died"

I want to cry,
and begin to fear.

Is this goodbye?
And shed a tear.

She says don't cry,
he's somewhere greater.

This isn't goodbye,
but a "see you later".

Way up high,
where I can't see

he's an angel in the sky,
waiting for me.

I won't see him next June,
but many Junes later.

All together one day,
with our creator.

So mama takes me outside,
at the clouds we stare.

She smiles and says,
"Your brother's up there."

About the Author
Jess Owen

Jess Owen knew she wanted to be an author at the young age of 8, and began writing little books in her room for fun. By age 10, Jess started winning awards, and her dreams of being an author grew. When Jess turned 13, she felt a strong calling from God to use her gift to spread the love of Jesus to children. She told God she would soon, but kept pushing it back. Then one night, Jess prayed to God that He would use her in ways she could never imagine possible. Withen a week, her family was faced with a potential financial crisis. While in the midst of chaos, Jess felt peace and knew God could use this to make something beautiful. Jess prayed and prayed, and finally God gave her His answer, which it what you're holding right now.

nstagram: @jessowen8

acebook: @jessowenbooks

www.ingramcontent.com/pod-product-compliance
Lightning Source LLC
Chambersburg PA
CBHW041819090426
42811CB00009B/1030